vegetablesides

vegetablesides

RYLAND
PETERS
& SMALL

LONDON NEW YORK

Designer **Luana Gobbo**

Commissioning Editor **Elsa Petersen-Schepelern**

Editor **Sharon Ashman**

Production **Patricia Harrington**

Art Director **Gabriella Le Grazie**

Publishing Director **Alison Starling**

First published in the United States in 2004
by Ryland Peters & Small, Inc.
519 Broadway, 5th Floor
New York, NY 10012
www.rylandpeters.com

10 9 8 7 6 5 4 3 2 1

Library of Congress Cataloging-in-Publication Data

Brown, Celia Brooks.
  Vegetable sides / by Celia Brooks Brown, Maxine Clark,
and Louise Pickford.
     p. cm.
  Includes index.
  ISBN 1-84172-721-0
  1. Cookery (Vegetables) 2. Side dishes (Cookery) I.
Clark, Maxine. II. Pickford, Louise. III. Title.
  TX801.B743 2004
  641.6'5--dc22

                              2004006100

Printed in China.

Notes

All spoon measurements are level.

Grills, ovens, and broilers should be preheated to the
required temperature—if using a convection oven, cooking
times should be reduced according to the manufacturer's
instructions.

contents

introduction

From greens to beans, squash to potatoes, vegetable sides add color, texture, and fresh flavors to a meal. Steamed vegetables are great, but sometimes it's appealing to jazz up your side dishes and cook something extra special. There's so much you can do to transform your vegetables— grill, broil, oven-bake, braise, or roast them. Cover them in a creamy, warming sauce, add fresh herbs, or marinate them to add flavor. However you like to cook them, there is a recipe here to suit, and lots of inspiration if you don't know where to start.

There are Italian, French, and Thai-inspired recipes, full of exciting flavors, as well as old favorites. Those people who aren't keen on vegetables will undoubtedly be tempted if you serve up these delicious ideas. They are a great way of increasing your family's intake of fresh vegetables, along with all the health benefits they bring.

Although most vegetables are available nearly all year round, think about using those that are local and seasonal in order to benefit from the best flavor and freshness. This book gives you ideas for every season, from something light and fresh for summer, such as Asparagus and Lemon with Smoked Garlic Mayonnaise, to something warm and soothing for winter, like Creamy Potato Gratin.

With vegetables dishes this tasty, why let them sit on the sidelines? Let them take center stage. In fact, many of the recipes would make great appetizers served on their own or as entrées options for vegetarians. So choose a recipe and make your vegetables the stars of the show!

beans, greens, & florets

green beans in tomato sauce

Good served hot or cold, this Italian recipe is stunning in its simplicity. It can be served as an accompaniment to an entrée or as an appetizer.

Put the olive and chile oils and garlic in a large saucepan and heat until the garlic has turned very lightly golden. Stir in the tomatoes, 1 cup water, and a large pinch of salt. Bring to a boil, then add the beans. Cover with a lid and cook gently for 30 to 40 minutes, stirring occasionally, until the beans are very tender.

¼ cup olive oil

1 teaspoon chile oil

1 garlic clove, crushed

two 16 oz. cans canned chopped tomatoes, 4 cups

1¼ lb. green beans, stems removed

sea salt

SERVES 4

Green beans are the classic accompaniment for lamb, but they are equally delicious with fish and chicken. You can also serve them at room temperature, as part of a salad buffet. Instead of the cooked beans, try long, thin slices of steamed zucchini, sautéed with the garlic.

green beans with garlic

1½ lb. green beans, trimmed

2 tablespoons extra virgin olive oil

1 tablespoon unsalted butter

2 garlic cloves, crushed

a handful of flat-leaf parsley, chopped

1 teaspoon freshly squeezed lemon juice (optional)

coarse sea salt and freshly ground black pepper

SERVES 4

Bring a large saucepan of water to a boil. Add the beans, return to a boil, and cook for 3 to 4 minutes. Drain and refresh under cold running water. Set aside.

Heat the oil and butter in a skillet. Add the garlic, cooked beans, and salt, and cook over high heat for 1 minute, stirring. Remove from the heat, then stir in the chopped parsley and lemon juice, if using. Sprinkle with pepper and serve.

Variation Flageolet beans are the other traditional partner for lamb. Generally, dried beans taste better if cooked from scratch rather than from a can, but this does require advance planning. Luckily, flageolets are the exception, especially if you can find imported French flageolets in jars, not cans. For mixed beans to serve with lamb (for four people), halve the quantity of green beans, and add a 14-oz. jar of drained beans to the cooked green beans when sautéing with the garlic. Instead of lemon juice, stir in 3 to 4 tablespoons crème fraîche or cream just before serving.

Beans were traditionally cooked this way in Tuscany when Chianti flasks were plentiful and blown from one piece of glass. The flask was embedded in the glowing ashes of the hearth to cook for as long as possible. You can use a casserole dish in the oven—it's just not as romantic.

beans simmered in a chianti flask

2½ cups small dried white beans (e.g., navy beans)

2 garlic cloves, unpeeled

6–8 fresh sage leaves

¾ cup extra virgin olive oil, plus extra for sprinkling

sea salt and freshly ground black pepper

a 2½-quart ovenproof casserole dish or beanpot, or a hand-blown Chianti flask and a roasting pan

a circle of waxed paper (see method), plus extra waxed paper or cheesecloth

SERVES 4

Put the beans in an ovenproof casserole dish or beanpot, or a hand-blown Chianti flask—don't use a modern molded flask with a seam, because it may crack. Add the whole unpeeled garlic cloves, sage, olive oil, salt, and pepper. Pour in enough warm water to fill the flask three-quarters full—or, if using a casserole dish or beanpot, pour in about 8 cups warm water.

Plug the neck of the flask with crumpled up waxed paper or with rolled and folded cheesecloth—this lets the contents "breathe" and stops the flask exploding. If using a casserole dish or beanpot, make sure it has a tight-fitting lid.

Put the flask on its side in a roasting pan half-filled with hot water and cook in a preheated oven at 325°F for 3 hours, turning every now and then. If using a casserole dish or beanpot, cover with a lid and put it in the oven, also at 325°F, and cook for 2 hours, then put a circle of waxed paper directly on top of the beans to keep in the moisture. Cover, and return to the oven to cook for another hour. The beans must be very tender and absorb most of the water and oil.

When cooked, transfer the beans to a heated serving dish and dress liberally with olive oil, then taste and season with salt and pepper. This dish is best served hot, with Italian sausages or roast pork, or as a simple appetizer with bread.

spinach flan

This recipe is inspired by a side dish from the Jura region of France, which was made from a glorious mixture of vegetables all thinly sliced and baked in a fabulous savory custard. Here, just spinach is used, but you could add a selection of vegetables of your choice, if you were feeling creative. It makes a particularly delicious accompaniment to roast pork.

Wash the spinach, then spin-dry in a salad spinner. Working in batches, heat 1 tablespoon of the oil in a nonstick skillet and add a mound of spinach. Cook the spinach over high heat, stirring until all the leaves have just wilted. Transfer to a plastic colander and let drain. Continue cooking until all the spinach has been wilted.

Chop the spinach coarsely. Put the sour cream, eggs, salt, and nutmeg in a bowl and beat well. Stir in the spinach.

Spread the butter over the bottom of the baking dish. Transfer the spinach mixture to the dish and bake in a preheated oven at 350°F until just set, 25 to 30 minutes. Serve hot.

1 lb. fresh spinach

3–5 tablespoons extra virgin olive oil

¾ cup sour cream or crème fraîche

2 large eggs

1 teaspoon coarse sea salt

a pinch of freshly grated nutmeg

1 tablespoon unsalted butter

a baking dish, about 12 inches long or about 8 inches diameter

SERVES 4

broccoli trees with pan-fried pine nuts

1 lb. broccoli, about
1 medium bunch

2 tablespoons butter

½ cup pine nuts

sea salt and freshly ground
black pepper

SERVES 4

Cut the broccoli into medium florets, leaving a long stalk. Put in a large, microwave-safe bowl, add ¼ cup water, cover with plastic wrap or a lid, and microwave on HIGH for 3 minutes. Alternatively, steam the broccoli for 4 to 5 minutes.

Meanwhile, put the butter, pine nuts, and salt and pepper to taste in a small saucepan. Cook over medium heat for 2 to 3 minutes, until the nuts are golden and the butter is foaming.

Drain the broccoli through a colander or strainer, return to the bowl, and toss with the pine nuts and butter. Serve immediately or let cool and serve as a salad.

This is about as speedy as good cooking gets! Broccoli is ideal for the microwave, as the stalks and florets cook evenly and don't go soggy.

A regular accompaniment on the *plat du jour* circuit in French bistros, this recipe goes especially well with pork. The secret of delicious cauliflower is to blanch it first; if you add a bay leaf to the water, the unpleasant cabbage aroma disappears.

cauliflower gratin

1 fresh bay leaf

1 large cauliflower, separated into large florets

2 cups heavy cream

1 large egg

2 teaspoons Dijon mustard

1½ cups finely grated Comté cheese, 6 oz.

coarse sea salt

a baking dish, about 10 inches diameter, greased with butter

SERVES 4–6

Bring a large saucepan of water to a boil, add the bay leaf, a generous shaking of salt, then add the cauliflower. Cook until still slightly firm, about 10 minutes. Drain and set aside.

Put the cream in a saucepan and bring to a boil. Boil for 10 minutes, then stir in the mustard and 1 teaspoon salt.

Divide the cooked cauliflower into smaller florets, then stir it into the cream sauce along with the egg. Transfer to the prepared baking dish and sprinkle the cheese over the top in an even layer. Bake in a preheated oven at 400°F until golden, about 40 to 45 minutes. Serve hot.

*Note Use Emmentaler, Cantal, or Swiss cheese if Comté is unavailable.

sardinian cauliflower with olives

This is a spectacular way to serve a whole creamy head of cauliflower—let your guests serve themselves, pulling out the florets. There's no fuss needed for this gloriously simple dish.

1 large whole cauliflower, green leaves removed and reserved

2 onions, finely chopped

1¼ cups small green pitted olives, about 10 oz.

⅓ cup olive oil, plus extra to serve

sea salt

a small bunch of flat-leaf parsley, finely chopped, to serve

SERVES 4

Line a large, heavy saucepan with the reserved outer leaves from the cauliflower. Put the cauliflower on top. Sprinkle with the onion, olives, and some salt, then pour the olive oil over it.

Cover with a lid, set over the lowest heat, and cook gently for about 40 minutes or until tender—there should be no resistance when a fork is inserted into the middle of the cauliflower.

Carefully lift the cauliflower out of the saucepan and onto a large plate—be very careful not to break it. Pile the onion and olives on top, then sprinkle with the parsley and more olive oil, and serve.

braised red cabbage
with chestnuts and apples

This red cabbage recipe includes apples, chestnuts, Alsatian Riesling, as well as bacon. Serve it with grilled or broiled sausages, pork chops, or roasts, and a glass or two of the same wine used in the cooking. It is also fantastic with Christmas goose.

1 red cabbage

3 tablespoons unsalted butter

1 onion, halved and thinly sliced

5 thick slices bacon, cut into thin slices

3 baking apples, peeled, cored, and chopped

7 oz. vacuum-packed whole peeled chestnuts

2 teaspoons coarse sea salt

1 cup dry white wine, preferably Riesling

1 tablespoon sugar

SERVES 4–6

Cut the cabbage into quarters, then core and slice thinly.

Melt 2 tablespoons of the butter in a sauté pan, big enough to fit the cabbage and other ingredients. Add the onion and bacon and cook until soft, about 3 minutes.

Add the remaining butter, the cabbage, apples, and chestnuts, and stir well. Season with salt, then add the wine, sugar, and 1 cup water.

Bring to a boil, continue to boil for 1 minute, then cover and simmer gently until the cabbage is tender, about 45 minutes. Serve hot.

This hybrid Thai coleslaw is based on the classic *som tum*, usually made from grated green papaya (when unripe, the fruit is firm, crunchy, and perfect for grating). Green papaya is not the easiest ingredient to find, so red cabbage is used here instead.

thai coleslaw

To make the dressing, reserve a few cilantro leaves, then put the rest in a blender or food processor. Add the chiles, garlic, soy sauce, lime juice, and sugar, and blend until smooth. Set aside.

Blanch the beans in boiling water for 2 minutes, then refresh in cold water. Mix the cabbage, beans, tomatoes, and scallions in a bowl. Pour the dressing on top, toss well to coat, and let marinate for about 30 minutes.

Spoon into bowls lined with the lettuce leaves, if using, sprinkle with the ground peanuts and the reserved cilantro leaves, then serve.

4 oz. green beans, trimmed, about 12–15 beans

2 cups finely shredded red or white cabbage

3 plum tomatoes, halved lengthwise, seeded, and sliced

4 scallions, sliced

⅓ cup roasted peanuts, coarsely ground

4 cup-shaped lettuce leaves, to serve (optional)

DRESSING

a handful of fresh cilantro

2 red serrano chiles, seeded

2 garlic cloves, chopped

2 tablespoons light soy sauce

2 tablespoons freshly squeezed lime juice

2 tablespoons palm sugar or soft brown sugar

SERVES 4

potatoes

calabrian-style potatoes and peppers

This is a fine example of the "less is more" approach to cooking—simple, good-quality ingredients cooked to perfection.

⅔ **cup olive oil**

1 red bell pepper, halved, seeded, and thickly sliced

1 yellow bell pepper, halved, seeded, and thickly sliced

1¼ lb. Yukon gold potatoes, thinly sliced (if unavailable, use russet or Idaho potatoes)

sea salt and freshly ground black pepper

a small bunch of flat-leaf parsley, finely chopped, to serve (optional)

SERVES 4

Heat the oil in a large, lidded skillet. Add the red and yellow peppers and cook for 10 minutes, stirring occasionally, until starting to turn golden brown. Add the potatoes, salt, and pepper, cover with a lid, and cook for 5 minutes.

Remove the lid and continue cooking for 15 minutes, turning every few minutes as the potatoes begin to brown, taking care not to break them. If the potatoes start to stick, this will just add to the flavor of the dish, but don't let them burn.

When the potatoes are tender, transfer to a serving dish and top with the parsley, if using. Let cool for 5 minutes before serving.

new potato salad
with gazpacho dressing

1 lb. baby new potatoes,
scrubbed but not peeled

GAZPACHO DRESSING

2 large, ripe tomatoes, halved,
seeded, and diced

2 oz. roasted red peppers
(from a jar), diced (about ⅓ cup),
alternatively, used diced pimiento

½ small red onion, chopped

1 garlic clove, chopped

3 tablespoons extra virgin
olive oil

2 teaspoons red wine vinegar

a pinch of sugar

a bunch of flat-leaf parsley,
coarsely chopped

sea salt and freshly ground
black pepper

SERVES 4

Gazpacho is the famous Spanish chilled soup, made with tomatoes, bell peppers, onions, and garlic. Use the same ingredients to make a fresh dressing for this simple salad of new potatoes. Add the dressing to the potatoes while they are hot, even if you aren't eating them right away, as this will help the flavors to infuse.

Bring a large saucepan of lightly salted water to a boil, add the potatoes, and return to a boil. Reduce the heat and simmer for about 12 minutes or until the potatoes are just tender when pierced with a knife.

Meanwhile, put the dressing ingredients in a large bowl and mix well. Add plenty of salt and pepper.

Drain the potatoes thoroughly and tip them into the dressing. Mix well and serve hot, or let cool to room temperature.

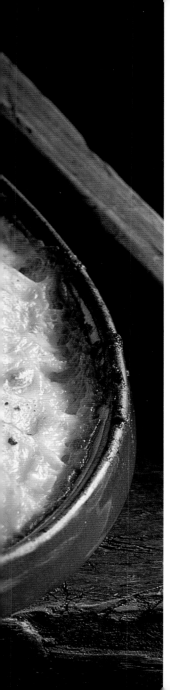

Cream and potatoes, mingling in the heat of the oven, are almost all you'll find in this well-loved dish. If it had cheese, it wouldn't be a true dauphinois. Serve as a partner for roast meat or poultry, with a mixed green salad, or simply on its own.

creamy potato gratin

4½ lb. boiling potatoes, cut in half if large

2 quarts whole milk

1 fresh bay leaf

2 tablespoons unsalted butter

2 cups whipping or heavy cream

a pinch of freshly grated nutmeg

coarse sea salt

a baking dish, 12 inches long

SERVES 4–6

Put the potatoes in a large saucepan, along with the milk and bay leaf. Bring to a boil, then lower the heat, add a pinch of salt, and simmer gently until partially cooked, 5 to 10 minutes.

Drain the potatoes. When cool enough to handle (but still hot), slice into rounds about ⅛ inch thick.

Spread the butter in the bottom of the baking dish. Arrange half the potato slices in the dish and sprinkle with salt. Top with the remaining potato slices and more salt. Pour the cream over the top and sprinkle with the grated nutmeg.

Bake in a preheated oven at 350°F until golden and the cream is almost absorbed, but not completely, about 45 minutes. Serve hot.

potato and mushroom gratin

Baking sliced potatoes and mushrooms in layers lets the potatoes absorb the juices and earthy flavor of the mushrooms. Use the darkest mushrooms you can find—they will have the best taste. You can always mix fresh mushrooms with reconstituted dried ones for a more intense flavor.

Peel the potatoes and slice thickly, putting them in a bowl of cold water as you go. Trim the mushrooms and slice thickly. Put half the potatoes in a layer in the bottom of the dish, sprinkle with olive oil, and cover with half the mushrooms.

Put the bread crumbs, Parmesan, parsley, salt, and pepper in a bowl and mix well. Spread half this mixture over the mushrooms, then sprinkle with more olive oil. Cover with a layer of potatoes, sprinkle with olive oil, then add a layer of the remaining mushrooms. Finally, sprinkle with the remaining bread crumb mixture and more oil.

Cover with foil and bake in a preheated oven at 350°F for 30 minutes. Uncover and cook for another 30 minutes, until the potatoes are tender and the bread crumb topping is golden brown.

Note If you blanch the potato slices first for 5 minutes in boiling salted water, they will need only 30 minutes uncovered in the oven.

2 lb. medium potatoes

1½ lb. flavorsome mushrooms such as portobello (or use fresh wild mushrooms)

extra virgin olive oil, for sprinkling

3½ cups stale (not dry) white bread crumbs

¼ cup freshly grated Parmesan cheese

¼ cup chopped fresh flat-leaf parsley

sea salt and freshly ground black pepper

a deep gratin or other ovenproof baking dish, well buttered

SERVES 4

roasted sweet potatoes
with shallots, garlic, and chiles

These crisp, golden, and bravely flavored sweet potatoes make a delicious alternative to regular roast potatoes. This recipe is for garlic- and chile-lovers everywhere.

12 shallots, unpeeled

8 garlic cloves, unpeeled

2 lb. orange-fleshed sweet potatoes, cut into even chunks

1 teaspoon coriander seeds, crushed

2 red serrano chiles

⅓ cup olive oil

sea salt and freshly ground black pepper

SERVES 4

Put the shallots and garlic in a bowl, cover with boiling water, let soak for 30 minutes, then drain and peel. The skins should slip off easily.

Transfer to a roasting pan and add the sweet potatoes, coriander seeds, and whole chiles. Add the olive oil, salt, and pepper, and toss well to coat.

Roast in a preheated oven at 400°F for 30 minutes until the potatoes are golden and tender. Shake the pan from time to time during cooking and brush the vegetables with the pan juices. Serve hot.

roots & stalks

asparagus and lemon with smoked garlic mayonnaise

The best way to enjoy asparagus is to roast or grill it. If you are using a charcoal grill, start cooking when the coals turn white, since this is when they are at their hottest. If using a stove-top grill pan, start cooking when the pan is smoking hot to maximize the asparagus flavor. To prepare asparagus, just snap off and discard the woody ends.

Heat an outdoor grill or stove-top grill pan until very hot.

Put the asparagus in a bowl, add the olive oil, and toss to coat. Set on the hot grill or grill pan, and cook for about 10 minutes, turning frequently, or until starting to become golden brown. Remove to a plate and sprinkle with salt and pepper. Squeeze the lemon juice over the top before serving.

Stir the smoked garlic into the mayonnaise and serve as an accompaniment.

24 asparagus spears

2–3 tablespoons olive oil

sea salt and freshly ground black pepper

freshly squeezed juice of ½ lemon, to serve

SMOKED GARLIC MAYONNAISE

3–4 smoked garlic cloves, crushed

¼ cup mayonnaise

SERVES 4

For this dish, you need beets and baby onions of roughly the same size, so they will cook evenly on the grill. They make an excellent accompaniment to meats or salads.

beet and pearl onion brochettes

32 large fresh bay leaves

20 small beets

20 pearl onions, unpeeled

3 tablespoons extra virgin olive oil

1 tablespoon balsamic vinegar

sea salt and freshly ground black pepper

8 metal skewers

SERVES 4

Put the bay leaves in a bowl, cover with cold water, and let soak for 1 hour before cooking.

Cut the stalks off the beets and wash well under cold running water. Bring a large saucepan of lightly salted water to a boil, add the beets and pearl onions, and blanch for 5 minutes. Drain, and refresh under cold running water. Pat dry with paper towels, then peel the onions.

Preheat an outdoor grill. Thread the beets, onions, and damp bay leaves onto the skewers, sprinkle with the olive oil and vinegar, and season well with salt and pepper. Cook over medium-hot coals for 20 to 25 minutes, turning occasionally, until charred and tender, then serve immediately.

Thyme is omnipresent in French cuisine. Here, it transforms ordinary boiled carrots into something subtly sumptuous. The cream helps, too. You can substitute steamed baby leeks for the carrots, but in that case, stir in a tablespoon or so of butter when adding the cream.

carrots with cream and herbs

2 lb. baby carrots, trimmed, or medium carrots

3 tablespoons unsalted butter

a sprig of thyme

2 tablespoons sour cream or crème fraîche

several sprigs of chervil

a small bunch of chives

fine sea salt

SERVES 4

If using larger carrots, cut them diagonally into 2-inch slices. Put in a large saucepan (the carrots should fit in almost a single layer for even cooking). Add the butter and set over low heat. Cook to melt and coat, about 3 minutes. Half-fill the saucepan with water, then add a pinch of salt and the thyme. Cover, and cook until the water is almost completely evaporated, 10 to 20 minutes.

Stir in the cream and add salt to taste. Using kitchen shears, snip the chervil and chives over the top, mix well, and serve.

Variation In spring, when turnips are sweet, they make a nice addition to this dish. Peel and quarter large turnips, or just peel baby ones and leave them whole—the main thing is to ensure that all the vegetable pieces (carrots and turnips) are about the same size so that they cook evenly. Use 3 to 4 cups carrots and 3 to 4 cups turnips, or double the recipe. Sprinkle with a large handful of just-cooked shelled peas before serving for extra crunch and color.

Tarator, the nut sauce served with these leeks, is found in Middle Eastern cooking, though cooks there would use ground almonds or walnuts. If the sauce is made in advance, beat it well before you use it.

1½ lb. baby leeks, trimmed

2–3 tablespoons extra virgin olive oil

sea salt

a few lemon wedges, to serve

TARATOR SAUCE

2 oz. macadamia nuts, toasted, about ½ cup

1 oz. fresh bread crumbs, about ½ cup

2 garlic cloves, crushed

½ cup extra virgin olive oil

1 tablespoon freshly squeezed lemon juice

2 tablespoons boiling water

sea salt and freshly ground black pepper

SERVES 4

charred leeks with tarator sauce

To make the sauce, put the nuts in a food processor and grind coarsely, then add the bread crumbs, garlic, and salt and pepper, and blend again to form a smooth paste. Transfer to a bowl and very gradually beat in the olive oil, lemon juice, and the 2 tablespoons boiling water to form a sauce. Season to taste with salt and pepper.

Preheat an outdoor grill or stove-top grill pan. Brush the leeks with a little olive oil, season with salt, and cook over medium heat for 6 to 10 minutes, turning occasionally, until charred and tender. Transfer to a plate, sprinkle with olive oil, pour the sauce over the top, and serve with the lemon wedges.

Fresh peas with lettuce form a classic of French cuisine. Teamed with asparagus in a light buttery sauce, they're ideal for serving with roast poultry or grilled fish. Bacon makes a nice addition so you can also stir in ¼ cup finely chopped sautéed bacon, just before serving. If chervil is unavailable, use finely chopped flat-leaf parsley instead.

asparagus, peas, and baby lettuce

6 tablespoons (¾ stick) unsalted butter

3–4 small shallots, sliced into rounds

2 romaine lettuce hearts, quartered

4 oz. asparagus tips, halved lengthwise, 1–1½ cups

2 cups shelled fresh peas, 2 lb. in the pod

coarse sea salt

sprigs of chervil or chives, snipped with kitchen shears, to serve

SERVES 4

In a saucepan with a lid, large enough to fit all the ingredients, melt half the butter. Add the shallots and lettuce and cook, covered, stirring often, until tender, 8 to 10 minutes.

Season with salt, add the remaining butter and the asparagus, and cook for 5 minutes.

Add the peas, cover, and cook for 3 more minutes. Taste for seasoning, sprinkle with the herbs, and serve.

Variation For a more substantial side dish, or even a light meal, add about 2 cups sliced baby carrots and a splash of water when cooking the lettuce. Bring another pan of lightly salted water to a boil, add 1 lb. small new potatoes, cook until tender, about 15 minutes, drain, then slice into wedges. Before serving, gently stir in a bit more butter or 1 tablespoon crème fraîche or sour cream into the asparagus and carrots, add the potato wedges, and serve.

Poor old celery; it is more often an ingredient than the star of a dish. However, in this traditional Provençal recipe, it takes center stage. Beef is the ideal complement to the trinity of celery, tomatoes, and anchovies, so serve this with roast beef or grilled steaks.

braised celery

2 whole bunches of celery

2 tablespoons extra virgin olive oil

2 thick slices of bacon, cut into thin strips

1 onion, quartered and sliced

1 carrot, quartered lengthwise and sliced

2 garlic cloves, sliced

1 cup canned chopped peeled tomatoes, 8 oz.

1 cup dry white wine

1 fresh bay leaf

8 canned anchovies, chopped

a handful of flat-leaf parsley, chopped

coarse sea salt and freshly ground black pepper

SERVES 4–6

Remove any tough outer stalks from the celery and trim the tips so they will just fit into a large sauté pan with a lid.

Bring a large saucepan of water to a boil. Add a pinch of salt, then the celery, and simmer gently for 10 minutes to blanch. Remove the celery, drain, and pat dry with paper towels.

Heat the oil in the sauté pan. Add the bacon, onion, and carrot, and cook gently until lightly browned. Add the celery and a little salt and pepper and cook until just browned, then remove the celery.

Add the garlic, cook for 1 minute, then add the tomatoes, wine, and bay leaf. Bring to a boil and cook for 1 minute. Add the celery, cover, and simmer gently for 30 minutes, turning the celery once.

Transfer the celery to a warmed serving dish. Raise the heat and cook the sauce to reduce it slightly, about 10 minutes. Pour it over the celery, sprinkle with the anchovies and parsley, and serve.

grilled corn on the cob

In this version of the famous recipe, corn on the cob steams inside the husks first, then has a short blast over hot coals to brown and flavor the kernels. Delicious served with this zesty herb butter.

4 ears of corn, unshucked

1¼ sticks butter

1 garlic clove, crushed

2 teaspoons chopped fresh thyme leaves

grated zest of 1 unwaxed lemon

sea salt and freshly ground black pepper

SERVES 4

Carefully peel back the husks from the corn, but leave them attached at the stalk. Remove and discard the cornsilk. Fold the husks back in position so the corn is covered again, and tie in place with twine. Put the corn in a large bowl of cold water, let soak for 30 minutes, then drain and pat dry with paper towels.

Preheat an outdoor grill, then cook the corn over medium-hot coals for 15 minutes, turning regularly until the outer husks are evenly charred. Remove from the heat, let cool slightly, then remove the husks. Return to the grill rack and cook for another 8 to 10 minutes, turning frequently until the kernels are lightly charred.

Meanwhile, put the butter, garlic, thyme, lemon zest, salt, and pepper in a small saucepan and heat gently until the butter has melted. Sprinkle the butter mixture over the cooked corn and serve.

tomatoes, eggplant, & squash

zucchini and tomatoes baked with fontina

Zucchini are much more flavorful when cooked this way—bathed in garlic and olive oil, then stuffed with sweet, ripe cherry tomatoes and enveloped in melting fontina cheese. Delightfully fresh and summery.

Cut the zucchini in half lengthwise and trim a little off the uncut sides so that they will sit still like boats. Using a teaspoon, scoop out the soft-seeded centers. Arrange the "boats", cut sides up, in a row in the prepared dish.

Put the garlic, olive oil, salt, and pepper in a bowl, stir well, then brush over the cut surfaces of the zucchini. Arrange the tomato halves in the grooves. Season well with salt and pepper, then sprinkle with olive oil and bread crumbs. Bake in a preheated oven at 325°F for 30 minutes.

Remove from the oven and arrange the cheese over the zucchini and tomatoes. Return the dish to the oven for another 10 minutes to melt the cheese. Serve immediately while the cheese is still bubbling.

6 medium zucchini (as straight as possible)

2 garlic cloves, chopped

2 tablespoons olive oil, plus extra for sprinkling

about 30 cherry tomatoes, halved

3–4 tablespoons dry bread crumbs

8 oz. fontina cheese, sliced, about 2 cups

sea salt and freshly ground black pepper

a shallow ovenproof dish, greased

SERVES 6

eggplant, tomato, and parmesan gratin

A pretty gratin bursting with flavor. Tomato halves are baked with briefly fried, thinly sliced eggplant and freshly grated Parmesan.

Cut the eggplant lengthwise into ¼-inch slices. Sprinkle with salt and let drain in a colander for 30 minutes. Rinse well and pat dry with paper towels. Cut the tomatoes in half through the middle.

Heat the oil in a skillet and sauté the eggplant in batches until deep golden brown. Drain on paper towels. Arrange a layer of eggplant in the prepared dish, then top with the tomato halves, cut side up. Sprinkle with the chopped basil, salt, pepper, and half of the Parmesan. Add another layer of eggplant, then the remaining Parmesan.

Bake the gratin in a preheated oven at 400°F for 25 to 30 minutes, or until browned and bubbling on top. Let cool slightly and serve warm, or let cool completely and serve as a salad.

1 large eggplant

1 lb. very ripe, red tomatoes, about 3 medium

about ⅔ cup olive oil

¼ cup chopped fresh basil

1¼ cups freshly grated Parmesan cheese

sea salt and freshly ground black pepper

a shallow ovenproof dish, well buttered

SERVES 4

beefsteak tomatoes with garlic and herb butter

To be enjoyed at their best, beefsteak tomatoes should be eaten hot, and preferably in season. They make a great focal point for any meal and their lack of pretension is hugely appealing.

Remove the stalk from each tomato and carefully cut out a small cavity for the filling.

Put the garlic, butter, chile oil, parsley, and pepper in a bowl and mix well. Fill the tomato cavities with the garlic mixture, pressing down gently as you go. Put on the baking tray, sprinkle with olive oil, and roast in a preheated oven at 300°F for 1 hour 20 minutes.

Remove from the oven and serve hot, with some of the cooking juices poured over the top.

4 beefsteak tomatoes

3 garlic cloves, crushed

6 tablespoons (¾ stick) unsalted butter, softened

1 teaspoon chile oil

a large handful of flat-leaf parsley, finely chopped

freshly ground black pepper

olive oil, for sprinkling

a baking tray

SERVES 4

ratatouille

2 lb. eggplant, cut into
1½-inch pieces

extra virgin olive oil (see method)

2 medium onions,
coarsely chopped

2 red bell peppers, halved,
seeded, and cut into
1½-inch pieces

2 yellow bell peppers, halved,
seeded, and cut into
1½-inch pieces

1 green bell pepper, halved,
seeded, and cut into
1½-inch pieces

6 smallish zucchini, about 1½ lb.,
halved lengthwise and sliced

4 garlic cloves, crushed

6 medium vine-ripened
tomatoes, halved, seeded,
and chopped

a small bunch of basil,
coarsely chopped

coarse sea salt

TO SERVE

a few basil leaves, thinly sliced

1 garlic clove, crushed

SERVES 4–6

This method for making ratatouille involves adding each vegetable separately, in the order which best suits their cooking requirements, rather than all at the same time. It does make a difference. It is also important to season each vegetable "layer" individually.

Put the eggplant pieces in a microwave-proof bowl with 3 tablespoons water and microwave on HIGH for 6 minutes. Drain and set aside.

Heat 3 tablespoons of oil in a deep sauté pan with a lid. Add the onions and cook until soft, 3 to 5 minutes. Salt lightly.

Add all the peppers and cook for 5 to 8 minutes more, stirring often. Turn up the heat to keep the sizzling sound going, but take care not to let it burn. Salt lightly.

Add 1 more tablespoon of oil and the zucchini. Mix well and cook for about 5 minutes more, stirring occasionally. Salt lightly.

Add 2 more tablespoons of oil and the drained eggplant. Cook, stirring often, for 5 minutes more. Salt lightly.

Add the garlic and cook for 1 minute. Add 1 more tablespoon of oil if necessary, and the tomatoes and basil, and stir well. Salt lightly. Cook for 5 minutes, then cover, lower the heat, and simmer gently for 30 minutes, checking occasionally.

Remove the pan from the heat. This is best served at room temperature, but it still tastes good hot. The longer you let it stand, the richer it tastes. Stir in more basil and garlic just before serving.

Turn ordinary vegetables into something fabulous with this gorgeous Thai-flavored sauce. Use it as a marinade here, but also try it as a ketchup—on burgers or on hot dogs. The sauce will keep for up to a week if kept in an airtight container in the refrigerator.

thai-glazed vegetable skewers

To make the Thai sauce, put all the sauce ingredients in a blender or food processor and blend until smooth.

Peel the mango with a sharp knife and stand it upright on a board, narrow end pointing up. Slice off thick cheeks parallel to the pit and cut off strips around the pit. Cut the flesh into equal chunks.

Thread the skewers with the fruit and vegetable chunks, each starting and ending with a lime leaf, if using. Brush the sauce generously over the loaded skewers, then cover and let marinate in the refrigerator for at least 30 minutes. Reserve the remaining sauce.

Put the skewers on a preheated outdoor grill or stove-top grill pan, or under a preheated broiler, and cook, turning occasionally and basting with the remaining sauce, until tender and lightly charred.

1 large, firm, ripe mango

1 yellow bell pepper, seeded and cut into 10 pieces

2 small red onions, cut into 10 wedges

2 small zucchini, cut into 10 pieces

1–2 limes, cut into 10 slices

10 button mushrooms

1 red bell pepper, seeded and cut into 10 pieces

5 serrano chiles, halved (optional)

20 kaffir lime leaves (optional)

THAI BARBECUE SAUCE

6 tablespoons coconut cream, or 3 tablespoons coconut milk powder mixed with 3 tablespoons water

⅛ cup dark soy sauce

2 tablespoons dark brown sugar

2 tablespoons rice wine vinegar or freshly squeezed lime juice

3 tablespoons tomato paste

3 kaffir lime leaves, chopped

1 lemongrass stalk, thinly sliced

1–2 bird's eye chiles, sliced

1 fat garlic clove, sliced

2 tablespoons sunflower oil

10 metal or long bamboo skewers (if bamboo, soak in water for 30 minutes)

MAKES 10

When pumpkin is in season, it often appears on menus as a gratin in the south of France. The conventional recipe is simply a purée with béchamel and a topping of crisp, browned bread crumbs. This version has rice, which gives it a more interesting texture and makes it substantial enough to be a meal on its own, served with a green salad.

pumpkin and rice gratin

Peel and seed the pumpkin and cut into small cubes. Put in a large saucepan with 2 tablespoons of the oil, a pinch of salt, and 1 cup water. Cook over low heat, stirring often and adding more water as necessary, until soft, about 20 to 30 minutes.

Meanwhile, put the rice and the remaining 1 tablespoon oil in another pan and cook over medium heat, stirring to coat the grains. Add 1 cup water, a pinch of salt, and the thyme sprig, and bring to a boil. Cover, and simmer until almost tender, about 10 minutes, then drain and discard the thyme.

Mix the bread crumbs with the parsley and a pinch of salt.

Squash the cooked pumpkin into a coarse purée with a wooden spoon and stir in the rice and sour cream. Taste; the topping and cheese will add flavor, but the pumpkin should be seasoned with salt and pepper as well.

Spoon the pumpkin mixture into the prepared baking dish and spread evenly. Sprinkle the cheese in a thin layer over the top, then follow with a layer of the bread crumbs. Bake in a preheated oven at 400°F until browned, about 20 to 30 minutes. Serve hot.

3 lb. pumpkin

3 tablespoons extra virgin olive oil

½ cup long-grain rice

a sprig of thyme

3 tablespoons fresh bread crumbs

a small handful of flat-leaf parsley, finely chopped

3 tablespoons sour cream or crème fraîche

¾ cup finely grated Gruyère or Swiss cheese, about 3 oz.

coarse sea salt and freshly ground black pepper

a large baking dish, greased with unsalted butter

SERVES 8

zucchini and patty pans infused with mint and balsamic vinegar

If you think that grilled food is predictable, this dish will change your opinion and prove to be a refreshing change. It looks and tastes sunny and fresh. You can prepare it in advance, then leave it for a couple of hours to soak up the oil, mint, and balsamic vinegar. Delicious.

Put the patty pans on a preheated outdoor grill or stove-top grill pan. Cook on each side for about 5 minutes or until tender, turning over when starting to brown.

When cooked, transfer to a serving dish. Pour the oil and vinegar over them and sprinkle with pine nuts, mint, salt, and pepper.

Cook the sliced zucchini on the grill or in the pan for 1 to 2 minutes each side. Add to the patty pan mixture and turn to coat. Cover, and let marinate for about 2 hours in the refrigerator, then serve.

Note Patty pans, also known as cymling and custard squash, are members of the squash family and are either yellow or green. They look a little alien, rather like mini flying saucers, but taste wonderful. They are available from large supermarkets all summer.

1 lb. yellow and green baby patty pan squashes, cut in half (or extra zucchini)

⅓ cup olive oil

2 tablespoons balsamic vinegar

½ cup pine nuts, about 2 oz., lightly toasted in a dry skillet

a handful of fresh mint leaves, coarsely chopped

3 zucchini (about 1 lb.), cut lengthwise into ⅛-inch slices

sea salt and freshly ground black pepper

SERVES 4

index

credits

RECIPES
Celia Brooks Brown
Thai coleslaw
Thai-glazed vegetable skewers
Roasted sweet potatoes
Maxine Clark
Zucchini and tomatoes baked with
fontina
Eggplant, tomato, and Parmesan
gratin
Potato and mushroom gratin
Beans simmered in a Chianti flask
Jane Noraika
Asparagus and lemon with
smoked garlic mayonnaise
Calabrian-style potatoes and peppers
Beefsteak tomatoes with garlic
and herb butter
Green beans in tomato sauce
Sardinian cauliflower with olives
Zucchini and patty pans with mint
Louise Pickford
Grilled corn on the cob
Beet and pearl onion brochettes
Charred leeks with tarator sauce
Laura Washburn
Braised celery
Asparagus, peas, and baby lettuce
Pumpkin and rice gratin
Creamy potato gratin
Carrots with cream and herbs
Green beans with garlic
Cauliflower gratin
Ratatouille
Braised red cabbage
Spinach flan
Lesley Waters
Potato salad with gazpacho dressing
Broccoli with pan-fried pine nuts

PICTURES
Martin Brigdale
Pages 1, 8–9, 14, 18, 22, 30–31,
40, 44, 46, 57, 61
Peter Cassidy
Endpapers, pages 4–5, 13,
16–17, 29, 33, 50–51, 53
Nicky Dowey
Pages 5, 6–7
William Lingwood
Pages 2, 10, 20–21, 26–27,
36–37, 62
Ian Wallace
Pages 39, 43, 49
Philip Webb
Pages 24–25, 34–35, 54–55, 58

conversion charts

Weights and measures have been rounded up
or down slightly to make measuring easier.

Volume equivalents:

American	Metric	Imperial
1 teaspoon	5 ml	
1 tablespoon	15 ml	
¼ cup	60 ml	2 fl.oz.
⅓ cup	75 ml	2½ fl.oz.
½ cup	125 ml	4 fl.oz.
⅔ cup	150 ml	5 fl.oz. (¼ pint)
¾ cup	175 ml	6 fl.oz.
1 cup	250 ml	8 fl.oz.

Weight equivalents: Measurements:

Imperial	Metric	Inches	Cm
1 oz.	25 g	¼ inch	5 mm
2 oz.	50 g	½ inch	1 cm
3 oz.	75 g	¾ inch	1.5 cm
4 oz.	125 g	1 inch	2.5 cm
5 oz.	150 g	2 inches	5 cm
6 oz.	175 g	3 inches	7 cm
7 oz.	200 g	4 inches	10 cm
8 oz. (½ lb.)	250 g	5 inches	12 cm
9 oz.	275 g	6 inches	15 cm
10 oz.	300 g	7 inches	18 cm
11 oz.	325 g	8 inches	20 cm
12 oz.	375 g	9 inches	23 cm
13 oz.	400 g	10 inches	25 cm
14 oz.	425 g	11 inches	28 cm
15 oz.	475 g	12 inches	30 cm
16 oz. (1 lb.)	500 g		
2 lb.	1 kg		

Oven temperatures:

225°F	(110°C)	Gas ¼
250°F	(120°C)	Gas ½
275°F	(140°C)	Gas 1
300°F	(150°C)	Gas 2
325°F	(160°C)	Gas 3
350°F	(180°C)	Gas 4
375°F	(190°C)	Gas 5
400°F	(200°C)	Gas 6
425°F	(220°C)	Gas 7
450°F	(230°C)	Gas 8
475°F	(240°C)	Gas 9